FROZEN : MUSIC FROM THE MOTION PICTURE

ISBN 978-1-4803-9612-8

Disney characters and artwork © Disney Enterprises, Inc.

WONDERLAND MUSIC COMPANY, INC.

DISTRIBUTED BY

HAL•LEONARD®
CORPORATION

7777 W. BLUEMOUND RD. P.O. BOX 13819 MILWAUKEE, WI 53213

In Australia Contact:
Hal Leonard Australia Pty. Ltd.
4 Lentara Court, Cheltenham, Victoria, 3192 Australia
Email: ausadmin@halleonard.com.au

Visit Hal Leonard Online at **www.halleonard.com**

C O N T E N T S

DO YOU WANT TO BUILD A SNOWMAN?

Music and Lyrics by KRISTEN ANDERSON-LOPEZ
and ROBERT LOPEZ

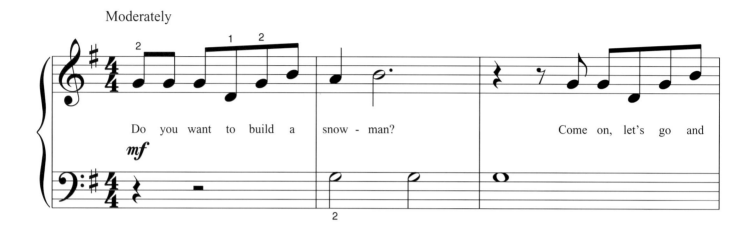

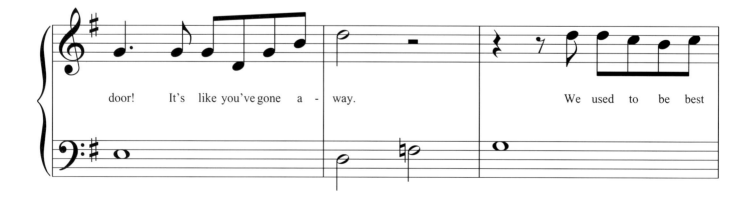

bud - dies, but now we're not. ___ I wish you would tell me

why. Do you want to build a snow - man?

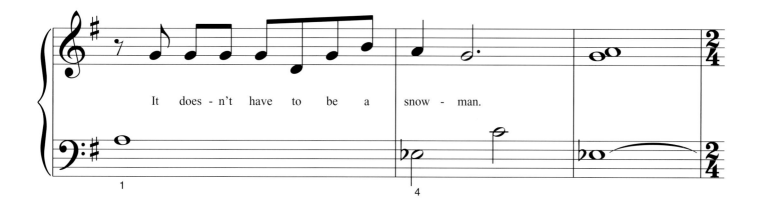

It does - n't have to be a snow - man.

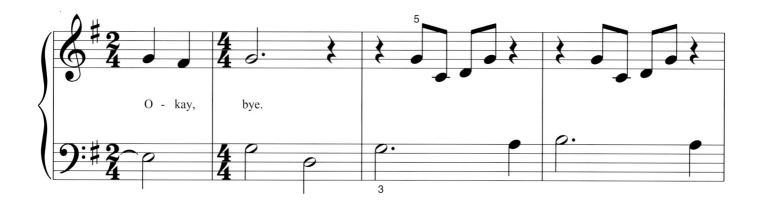

O - kay, bye.

6

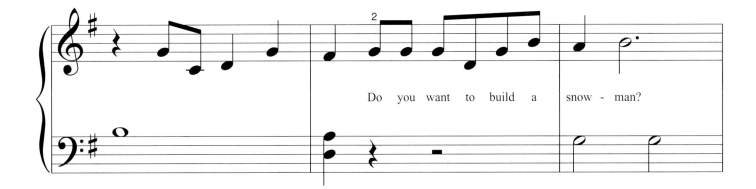

Do you want to build a snow - man?

Or ride our bikes a - round the halls? I think some com - pan - y is

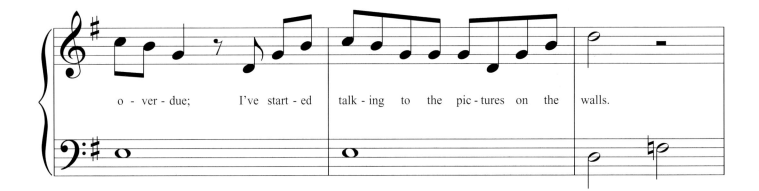

o - ver - due; I've start - ed talk - ing to the pic - tures on the walls.

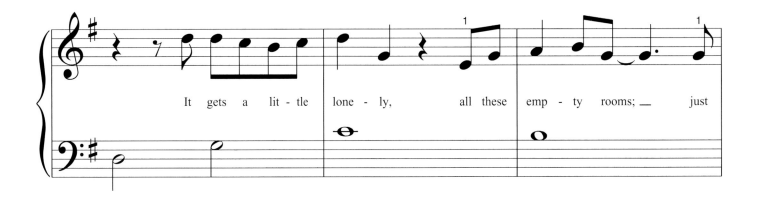

It gets a lit - tle lone - ly, all these emp - ty rooms; just

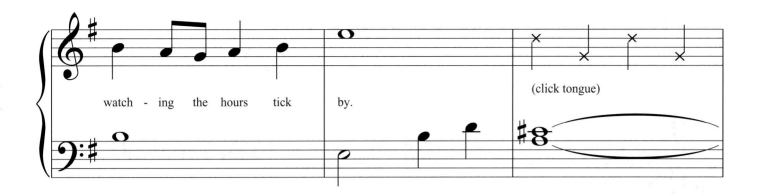

watch - ing the hours tick by.

(click tongue)

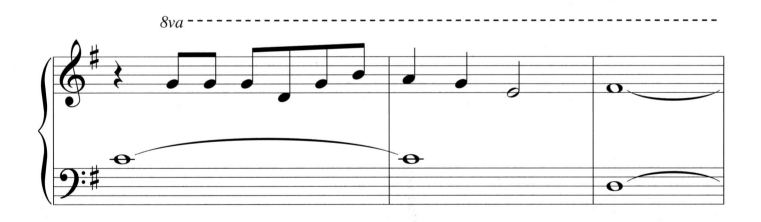

Do you want to build a snow - man?

8va -

(8va) -

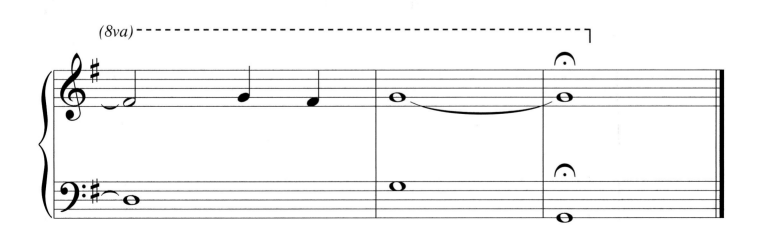

FOR THE FIRST TIME IN FOREVER

Music and Lyrics by KRISTEN ANDERSON-LOPEZ
and ROBERT LOPEZ

With excitement

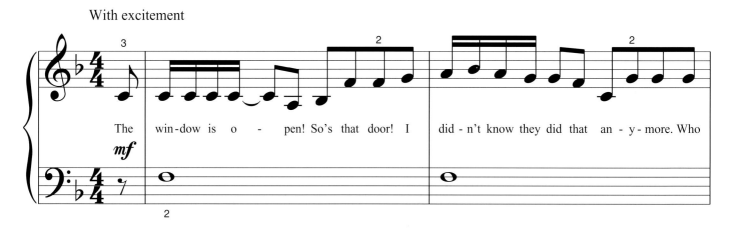

The win-dow is o - pen! So's that door! I did - n't know they did that an - y - more. Who

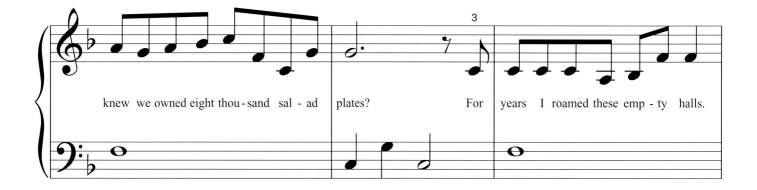

knew we owned eight thou-sand sal - ad plates? For years I roamed these emp - ty halls.

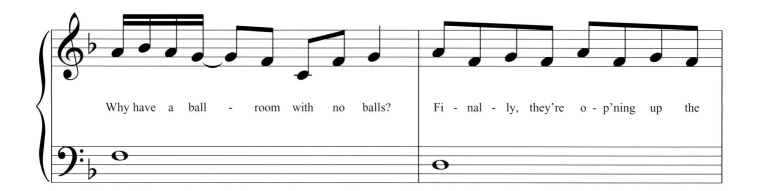

Why have a ball - room with no balls? Fi - nal - ly, they're o - p'ning up the

gates! There'll be ac - tual real live peo - ple;

it'll be to - tal - ly strange. But, wow! Am I so read - y for this

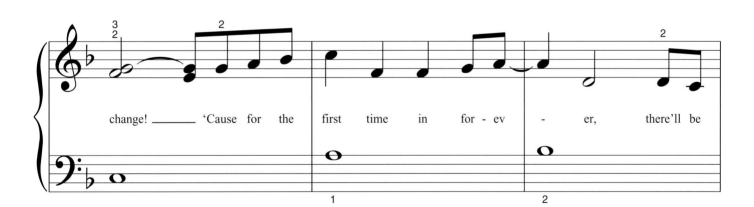

change! _____ 'Cause for the first time in for - ev - er, there'll be

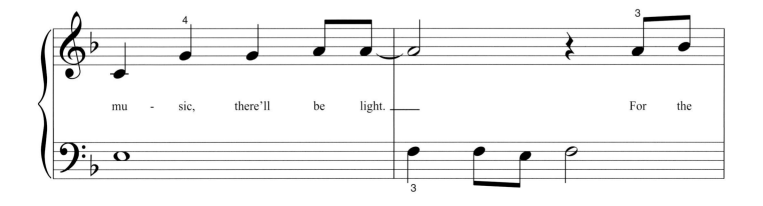

mu - sic, there'll be light. _____ For the

first time in for-ev - er, I'll be danc - ing through the

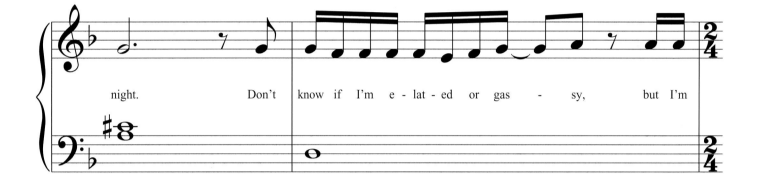

night. Don't know if I'm e - lat - ed or gas - sy, but I'm

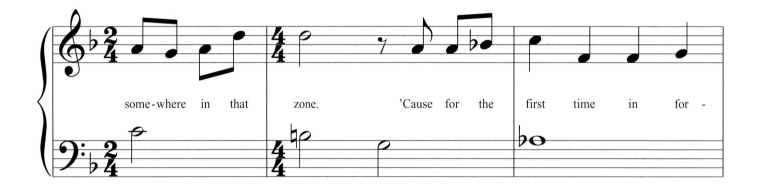

some-where in that zone. 'Cause for the first time in for -

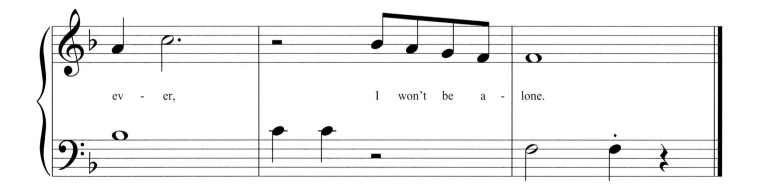

ev - er, I won't be a - lone.

LOVE IS AN OPEN DOOR

Music and Lyrics by KRISTEN ANDERSON-LOPEZ
and ROBERT LOPEZ

Moderately slow

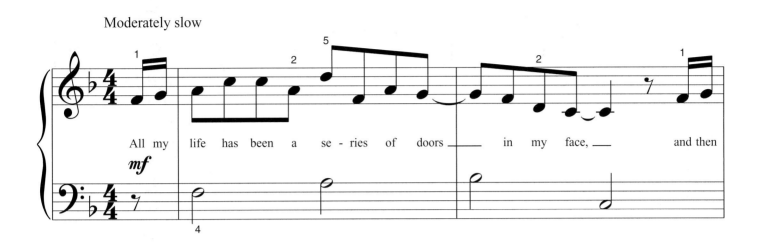

it's the par - ty talk - ing, or the cho - c'late fon - due. ____ But with you, __

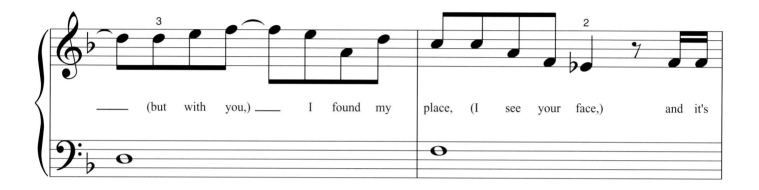

__ (but with you,) ____ I found my place, (I see your face,) and it's

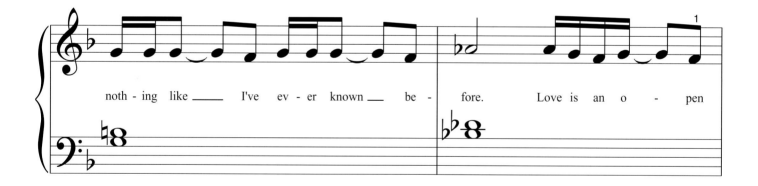

noth - ing like ____ I've ev - er known ___ be - fore. Love is an o - pen

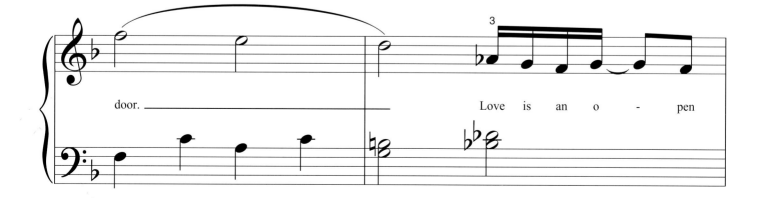

door. ____ Love is an o - pen

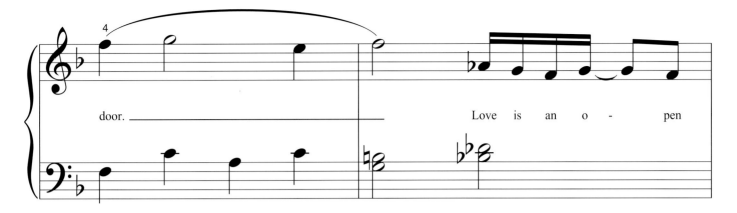

door. _____ Love is an o - pen

door with you, (with you,) with you! (With you!) Love is an o - pen

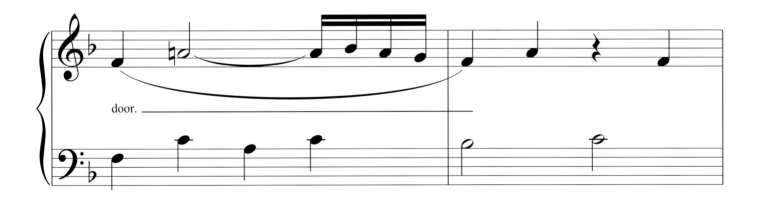

door. _____

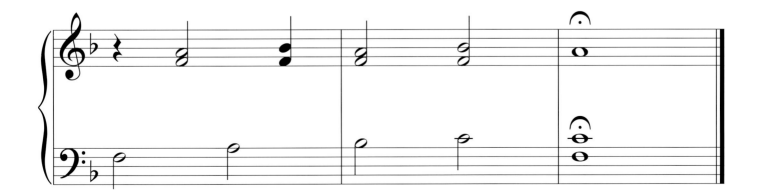

LET IT GO

Music and Lyrics by KRISTEN ANDERSON-LOPEZ
and ROBERT LOPEZ

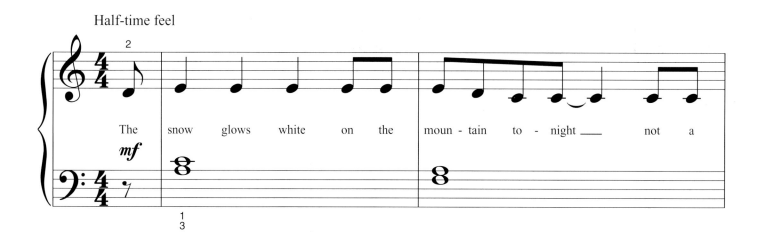

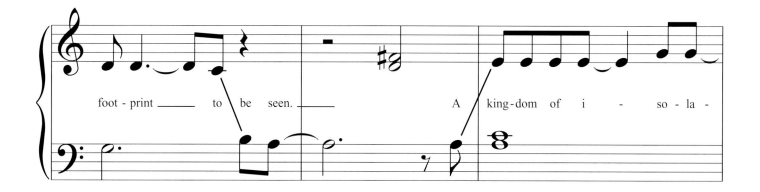

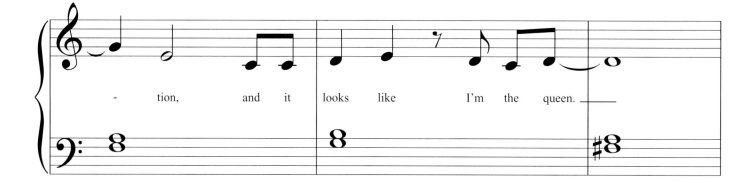

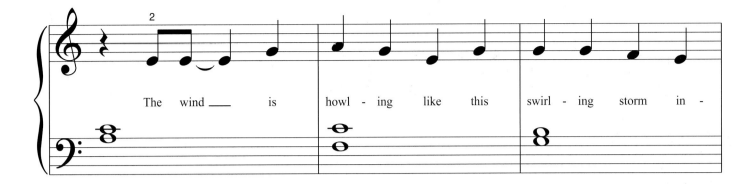

The wind ___ is howl - ing like this swirl - ing storm in -

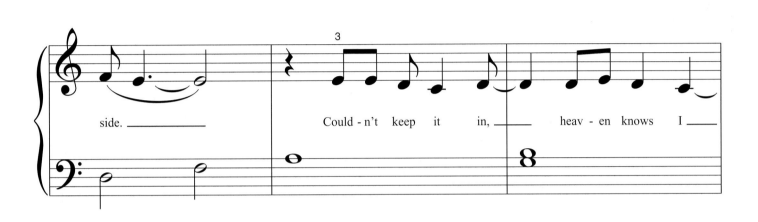

side. _____ Could - n't keep it in, ___ heav - en knows I ___

___ tried. Don't let ___ them

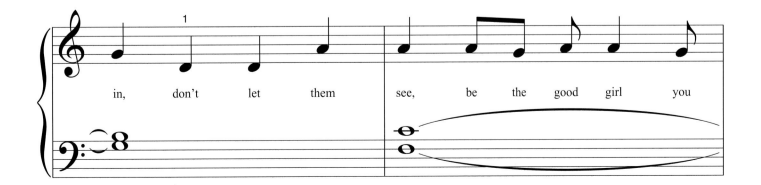

in, don't let them see, be the good girl you

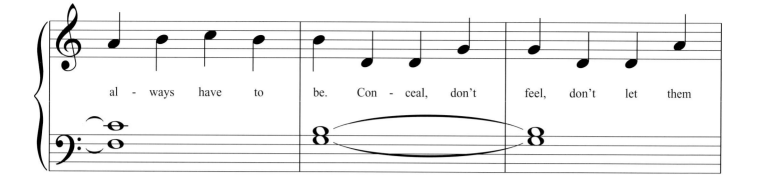

al - ways have to be. Con - ceal, don't feel, don't let them

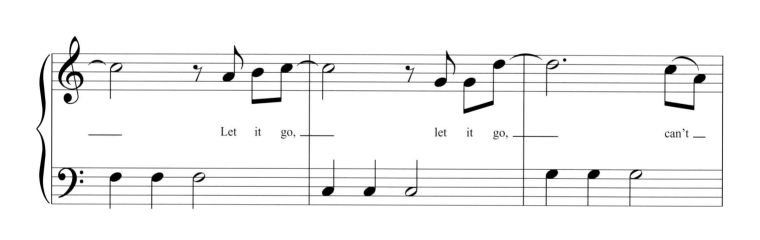

know... Well, now they know.

Let it go, let it go, can't

hold it back an - y - more. Let it go, let it go,

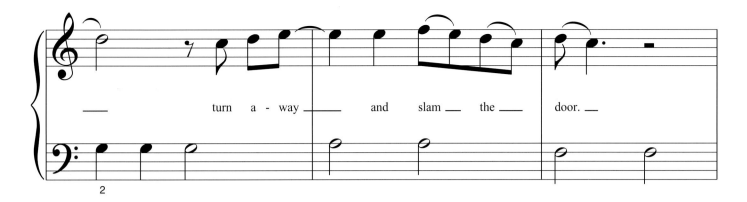

turn a - way _____ and slam ____ the ____ door. ____

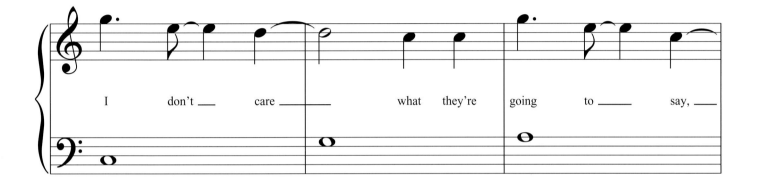

I don't ____ care _____ what they're going to ____ say, ____

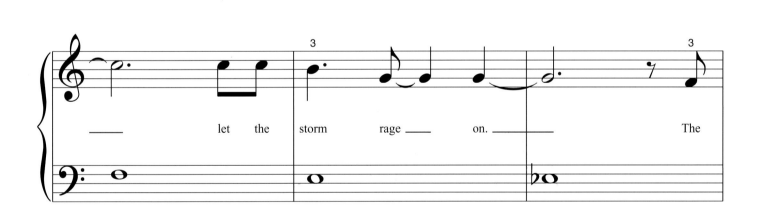

____ let the storm rage ____ on. ____ The

cold nev - er both - ered me an - y - way. ____

IN SUMMER

Music and Lyrics by KRISTEN ANDERSON-LOPEZ
and ROBERT LOPEZ

sum-mer. ___ I'll fi - n'lly see a sum-mer breeze ___ blow a - way a win-ter storm, ___ and

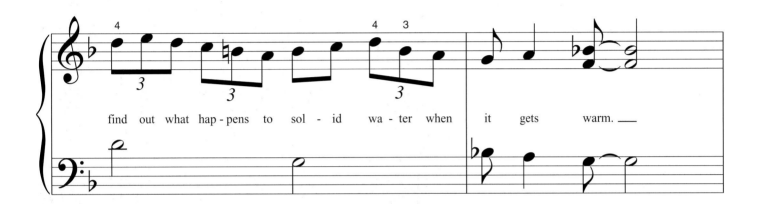

find out what hap-pens to sol - id wa - ter when it gets warm. ___

And I can't wait to see what my bud-dies all think of me. Just im-

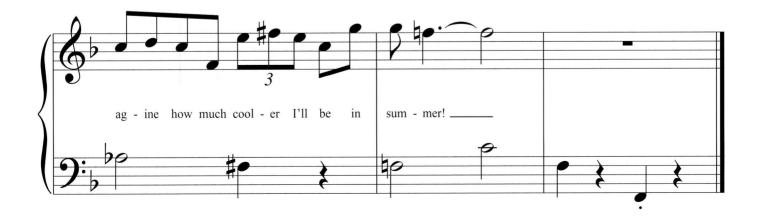

ag - ine how much cool - er I'll be in sum - mer! _____

FIXER UPPER

Music and Lyrics by KRISTEN ANDERSON-LOPEZ
and ROBERT LOPEZ

With comic bounce

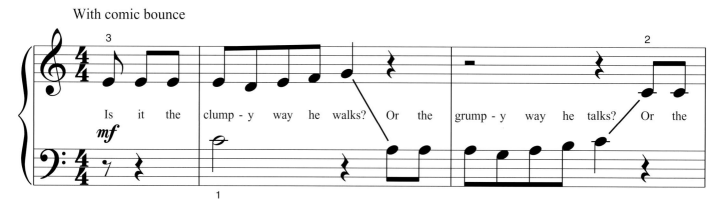

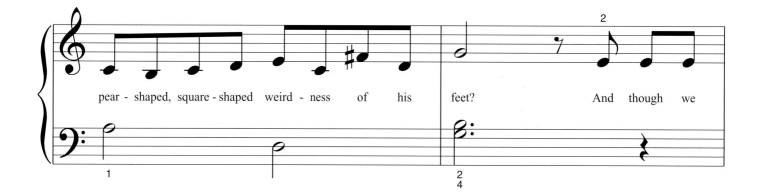

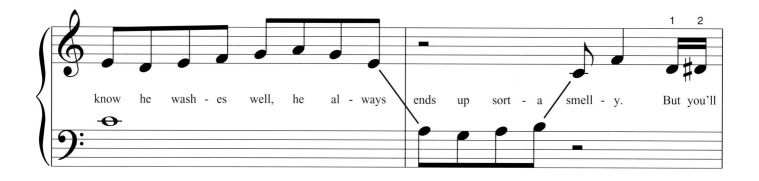

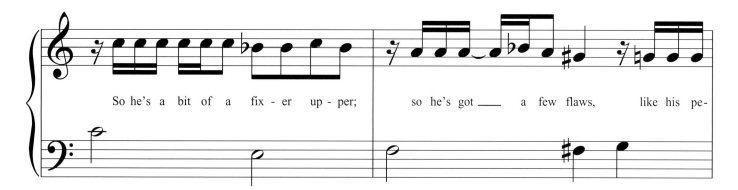

So he's a bit of a fix - er up - per; so he's got ___ a few flaws, like his pe-

cu - liar brain, dear, his thing with the rein - deer, that's a lit - tle out - side of na - ture's laws!

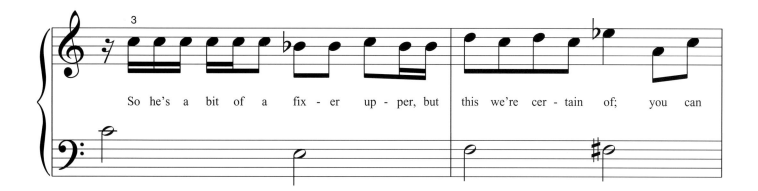

So he's a bit of a fix - er up - per, but this we're cer - tain of; you can

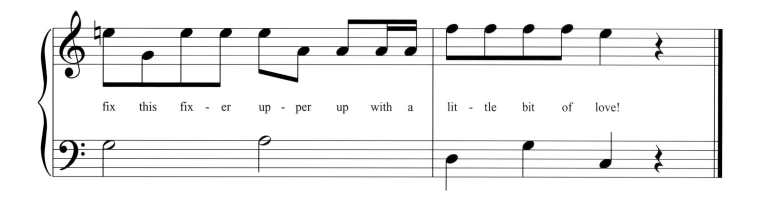

fix this fix - er up - per up with a lit - tle bit of love!

REINDEER(S) ARE BETTER THAN PEOPLE

Music and Lyrics by KRISTEN ANDERSON-LOPEZ
and ROBERT LOPEZ

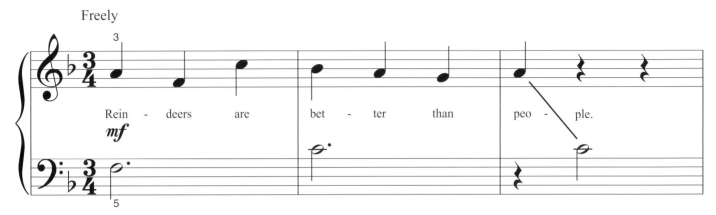

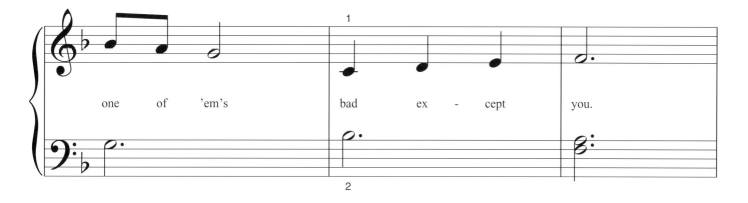

one of 'em's bad ex - cept you.

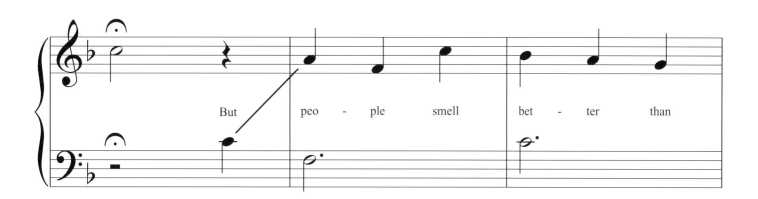

But peo - ple smell bet - ter than

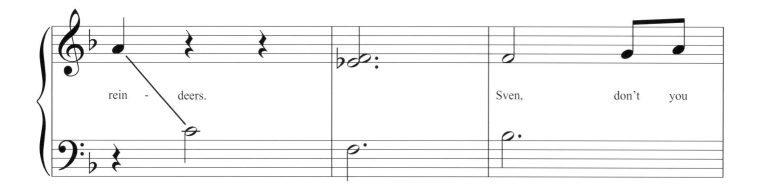

rein - deers. Sven, don't you

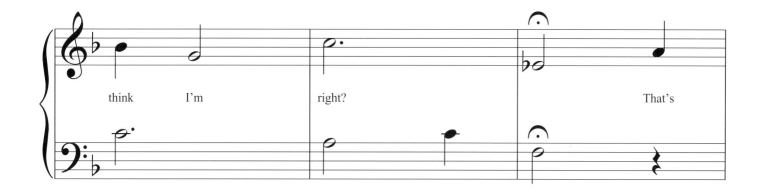

think I'm right? That's

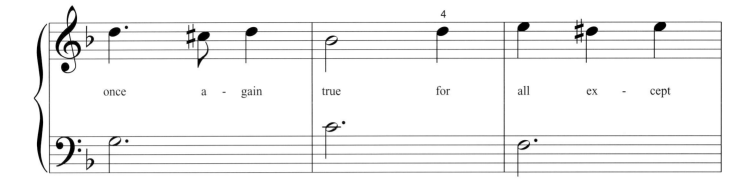

once a - gain true for all ex - cept

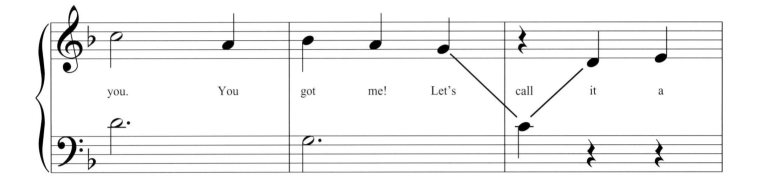

you. You got me! Let's call it a

night. Good night! Don't let the

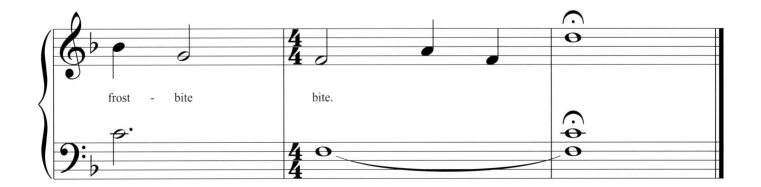

frost - bite bite.